SENIOR (still) LIVING

BY JOYCE DANIELS GROSS

Illustrations by Dani Kates

ISBN-13: 9798607255596

Edited by Patrick Gross
Illustrations by Dani Kates

facebook.com/SeniorStillLiving/

Joyce Gross
January 2 at 1:04PM

Preface

For some time, I have been posting items on social media about senior living and I now have a following of over nineteen people, two of whom have actually commented that I try for a wider audience.

I feel that I am qualified by virtue of having been the editor of my high school newspaper from 1947-1948, and in addition over the last seventy years having taken several hours of writing classes. Best of all for the last seven years I have actually been living independently in my senior residence where I can graduate into assisted living and memory care in this very same building! So, I know whereof I speak. ("Whereof" being a perfectly good word not commonly used these days ... so get used to it, I am 89!)

👍 Like   💬 Comment   ↗ Share

Joyce Gross
January 5 at 7:58AM

Moving In

In addition to downsizing when I moved into a brand-new Senior Residence, I underwent a perspective change. The administrator welcomed me and said, "Consider this your home now," so I did. Instead of an apartment, I have a luxurious bedroom suite complete with a full kitchen, a living room and a large bathroom that has a shower big enough to hold a small vehicle.

Because of my new thinking, I also have a chef and a dining room with fresh tablecloths on the tables every day. I have an exercise room complete with a trainer, a library, a billiard room, an arts and crafts room and a cozy theater for my viewing pleasure. Of course, for amusement I have a club room for card games, and it has a lovely bar (BYOB, but still.) And best of all being in Minnesota, IT HAS A HEATED GARAGE!

👍 **Like**   💬 **Comment**   ➢ **Share**

Joyce Gross
January 11 at 11:04AM

Money

I was checking with one of my sons about my retirement funds. He was consulting actuarial tables when he said, "How long do you think you will live?" We almost died laughing. Now that would certainly have screwed up the actuarial tables.

👍 **Like**   💬 **Comment**   ↪ **Share**

Joyce Gross
January 16 at 10:30AM

Doctor

I went to the doctor yesterday to get a shot of cortisone in my elbow. She asked why I had waited so long (five years). I told her I did not realize how bad it was hurting until I picked up a gallon of detergent. Then I explained to her that it was like a frog in a pot of cold water. You turn up the heat and before the frog realizes it's in trouble, he's cooked.

She did not get it, but all the time her brain was processing it and then she said that maybe the orthopedic doctors could use the reverse of that and convince their patients that they could tolerate some pain before they become addicted to opioids. Yet another medical breakthrough from my generation. You're welcome! I am interested in all things medical because I was, am, still, but not so much a nurse. As a nurse of my generation, the first phrase I was taught was "you are fine." I raised my seven kids that way. Although I still let them stay home from school when they were contagious and I guess they did get waited on by me and from what their spouses tell me, they still expect it.

The other two things I remember was the nun preparing us for floor duty for the next three years who said, "Never stand when you can sit and never sit

[see more]

when you can lie down." I took that to heart. The other thing I remember was being scared to death about taking narcotics and having to count every single pill every eight-hour shift when you carried the Narcotic Key! I now get nervous about taking a Tylenol. The other thing I learned about that time, I never knew how much a leg weighed until I had to carry one down to the pathology lab. But I digress.

👍 **Like**   💬 **Comment**   ↪ **Share**

Joyce Gross
January 22 at 8:13AM

Between the Sheets

If I am ever found dead in my Senior Living apartment you will have found me in my bedroom with my arm caught against the wall and my bed trying to put a fitted sheet on my 940-pound mattress.

The sheet has been cunningly designed by a young person who thought that yards of fabric interlaced with myriad rows of elastic was a fabulous idea. Never mind that the fabric reaches 20 inches under a mattress that I cannot lift.

Yes, I could get an air or foam mattress or use flat sheets and never tuck anything in again. It may come to that.

👍 **Like**   💬 **Comment**   ↪ **Share**

Joyce Gross
January 29 at 4:52PM

Book Club

You really get to know someone through a book club. Luckily, I belong to two of them. My old neighborhood group and the one I lead here in my establishment. You would be surprised at the difference in perspective between a 60-some year old and a 93-year- old reading the same book. Too much sex and nasty words and far-out plots that do not make sense, too many characters, too much going back and forth and that is just from the younger group. Needless to say, our discussions are profound and hilarious!

My generation went from "Frankly, Scarlet, I don't give a damn," the first curse word ever spoken in a movie, to sentences in books and movies with four F-words in every sentence. We must improve the rhetoric.

Really do you want to see your Grandma and Grandpa's headstones reading "What the F- - -"?

👍 Like   💬 Comment   ↪ Share

Joyce Gross
February 3 at 7:30AM

Snow
Fresh baked cookies, coffee, and tea are available every day in our Senior Living establishment, but ever since it started snowing, I have been hankering for homemade chocolate no-bake cookies. I needed cocoa, sugar, walnuts, coconut, peanut butter, oatmeal, and butter.

I found two boxes of cocoa: one sell-by date in 2016, the other opened one from 2017. The unsalted butter looked suspicious. It was yellow on the out-side but white inside. The unopened bag of coconut sell-by date was in November 2017.

The sugar was fine after I broke up the clumps and there was enough peanut butter in the bottom of the jar to make a half cup. The walnuts and oatmeal were from this year.

I made it anyway. You know why? BECAUSE THIS IS WHAT MINNESOTA HOUSEWIVES DO WHEN THEY ARE SNOWED IN FOR THREE DAYS. Yum!

👍 **Like**   💬 **Comment**   ↪ **Share**

Joyce Gross
February 8 at 8:15AM

Yoga
After many months our Yoga class is proficient in the following poses: Volcano, Boat, Cat, Flying Monkey, Cow, Warrior, and Downward Dog.

We are even able to do all this while sitting in chairs!

👍 **Like**   💬 **Comment**   ↪ **Share**

Joyce Gross
February 10 at 1:24PM

The Aquarium Senior Centers often have aquariums. We got ours a couple weeks ago. Actually, we got the container, the coral, caves and supposedly six shy goldfish but I have only seen the one who hides out in the tiny cave at the bottom of the aquarium. As I approach, he swims backwards into the cave surprising me as I did not know that fish swim backwards and had really not thought about it until now.

The other five fish have been hiding and almost no one has seen them. Apparently, the six are the canaries in the coal mine and if they make it others will come.

Today one of the retired teachers explained to me that female fish's heads swell up when they are full of eggs and they spew them out of their heads all over when she lays them. I do not believe this. Another friend says she was at her doctor's office waiting room gazing at their aquarium when she observed a large fish chasing a smaller fish and actually eat it. She was horrified and reported it to the person at the desk who reassured her by saying, "Oh, yes, that happens all the time."

My friend says she will never look at our aquarium! This whole aquarium business has opened a whole new world for me. I can hardly wait to see the eggs bursting forth from the heads of pregnant goldfish and am waiting to see the big fish gobbling down the little fish. It is kind of like being at the Lake.

 Like    **Comment**   **Share**

Joyce Gross
February 15 at 11:03AM

Cardio

1. Workout with weights … 55 minutes.

2. Drink water … eat cookie.

3. Nap.

👍 **Like**   💬 **Comment**   ↪ **Share**

Joyce Gross
February 18 at 7:08AM

Breakfast
The most important meal of the day serves four important functions.

1. We are still here: this undoubtedly is the most important accomplishment of the day.

2. Meet and Greet: we arrive fully dressed and may or may not speak to fifteen to twenty people. This is called socializing and apparently it is very important to old people.

3. Security: who did not show up? This engenders much discussion about doctor appointments and the reasons for them sleeping in, or who doesn't want to socialize. As a last resort, after breakfast, we go and knock on doors to check on number 1.

4. Food.

👍 Like   💬 Comment   ↪ Share

Joyce Gross
February 25 at 3:42pm

Rust

My 1948 High School class motto: If You Rest You Rust! I did not know until I moved in here and saw an older woman dusting her 27-year-old Lexus with 190,000 miles on it that people actually did that. Apparently, it pays off as there was not a speck of rust on the Lexus—and she lived in Minnesota all her life.

My granddaughter said to me, "Grandma, I never thought I would see you drive a car with rust on it."

I'm only a year away from 90 and I may give up driving then, so perhaps I need to start dusting!

👍 **Like**   💬 **Comment**   ↪ **Share**

Joyce Gross
March 3 at 10:56AM

Shopping

Now that I am in Senior Living, I'm really getting around. I can shop at three different grocery stores. I can go to different restaurants every week, the Guthrie Theatre, Flower Show, Farmers Market, Apple Orchard Library, and the Arboretum. And why, you ask, do I have this flurry of activity at my age? We have a bus!

👍 **Like**   💬 **Comment**   ↱ **Share**

Joyce Gross
March 9 at 2:30PM

Drainage

Today I had the environmental engineer come up to fix my slow draining bathroom sink and shower. After he left, I looked under the shower bench and saw a mass of black dirt and grit. It seemed like a good idea at the time, but I promise to never again use the detachable shower head to clean the floor mat from my car. Or maybe I should vacuum it first?

👍 **Like**   💬 **Comment**   ↪ **Share**

Joyce Gross
March 15 at 5:18PM

Tattoos

I can't help wondering when I look at the stunning dresses from the Met Gala what the tattoos on those beautiful women will look like when they are 89 years old. I do not know anyone at my establishment with a tattoo now, but I will keep checking as warmer weather arrives.

 Like    Comment   Share

Joyce Gross
March 23 at 8:47AM

Food

Those of us who are still Independent and do our own cooking for lunch and dinner talk endlessly about food. We reminisce about the fabulous cooking we did in bygone days, true or not, for families and spouses. We talk about the wonderful recipes and the endless Christmas cookies and the foods for special holidays. We remember when we polished silver twice a year, which our kids don't want to inherit! We remember when everyone canned crates of peaches and pears and bushels of tomatoes, varieties of pickles and relishes, and jams and jellies. We recall how everything changed with a freezer just as we remembered what an electric refrigerator did to the ice boxes. When we close our eyes, we remember what the ice tasted like on a hot summer day when we scrambled for the shards falling from the block of ice as it was cut to size in the ice wagon.

But this is now, and we must move forward, so we trade ideas about shorter recipes and frozen foods and cooking shortcuts and of creative ideas for leftovers! We are not too removed from our grandchildren out on their own for the first time figuring out how to feed themselves. We are young like that!

 Like    Comment   Share

Joyce Gross
March 27 at 9:24AM

AARP

I was just reading an AARP magazine which you are insulted to receive in the mail when you are just in your 50s. It was an article about the body changes you get in your 70s. Hahaha, I thought, just wait until you are 89. However, I like reading about the 70 and up youngsters they were referring to in the article. They pointed out the beneficial exercise you can get by having a dog you need to walk several times a day.

Upon reading that I got another of my brilliant ideas for the age of technology. We need to make a cute reasonably priced soft cuddly robot dog for our age group. It must have an easily programmable leash with which we can walk the dog several times a day. Since we already spend a great deal of time keeping ourselves neat and tidy, we can skip the part of real pets needing wiping, bending, scooping plus going outside on frigid Minnesota nights.

The dog should be programmed to perform simple tricks for the people we encounter, causing socializing, which apparently enhances older people's longevity. The best part is now we won't be thought of as talking to ourselves as we can say we are calling

[see more]

Piri, who I have named for the Siri to pets. We know how easily we can be persuaded to buy these robotic dogs as we remember how easily people were programmed to carry around pet rocks.

 Like    Comment   Share

Joyce Gross
March 28 at 8:44PM

Inside Family, Outside Family
When you first move into Senior Living everyone looks so old. It takes a while and an unexpected glance into a mirror to let you know that you are not looking so dang young yourself. You begin to share stories with people who are different from you. They are from New York, Florida, North Carolina, Seattle, Kentucky, California, Arizona, Chicago, Hawaii, Africa, Russia, Norway, Ukraine, and even Iowa (little joke). Why do these individuals come here? Because their kids live close by. You find out all families are alike, and this is now your Inside Family. You already know who your Outside Family and friends are. What is great about this? You have just doubled your Family. Why is this good, you ask? Because when you get mad at one family you can go talk about it to your other family and they will GET IT!

👍 Like   💬 Comment   ↪ Share

Joyce Gross
April 1 at 6:10PM

From Stereoscope to 3D Avengers Infinity War
Yes, of course, I saw the Avengers movie. It is after all kind of a family business. The last time I saw a 3D picture was in 1937 when I saw a picture on a stereoscope (Google it).

Lying on a recliner in the second row with special glasses on over my glasses I was surprised at how much I really liked Spider Boy Man. He is like everyone's teenager except for the fact that he is so sticky and too big for my lap which I realized when he actually hurtled toward me. This is actually a whiz bang extravaganza of a movie. I liked it. I really, really liked it.

👍 **Like**   💬 **Comment**   ↪ **Share**

Joyce Gross
April 8 at 7:44AM

Paranoia

As we residents age in this establishment paranoia abounds. The stolen purse turns up in the oven, the missing jewelry hides in the jar of jewelry cleaner, and the toilet paper was not stolen out of the bathroom. I got an early start in possible theft of items when my young children found my missing eyeglasses in the refrigerator.

 Like    Comment   Share

Joyce Gross
April 12 at 10:30PM

Happy Hour

"Consider this your home" the Executive Director stated as she welcomed the original dozen of us who moved into our brand new building. The first thing we new residents started was Happy Hour, or as the powers that be later suggested, "Social Hour."

I still call it Happy Hour. Social hour sounds to me like a Ladies Aid Society meeting at Church. It's not so much that, but how happy can you really get from 4:00 to 5:00 p.m. once a week? Therefore, a smaller group of us also meet on Mondays and Wednesdays at 4:00 p.m. We call ourselves the Winos. Not politically correct either.

👍 **Like**   💬 **Comment**   ↷ **Share**

Joyce Gross
April17 at 9:08PM

Happy Hour Revisited
What happens at social Happy Hour? Friday from 4:00 to 5:00 p.m. has been a hit at our establishment. We start out orienting ourselves by realizing another Friday is here and that our aging parents were indeed right about how fast time goes when you are old. We refresh ourselves with whatever we have brought to drink, and so many people now bring snacks that sometimes we do not have to eat any dinner. Whoever might want to read words of wisdom or update us on anything of general interest has the microphone.

We love old people jokes. I get mine from cousin-once-removed Tim in Texas who takes time from his busy law practice to forward them to me. Like this senior pickup line: an elegant older gentleman comes into a bar and spots a very classy 75-year-old woman sitting alone. He sits next to her, orders a drink, takes a sip and says, "So do I come here often?" That really cracks us up!

👍 **Like**   💬 **Comment**   ↪ **Share**

Joyce Gross
April 23 at 2:24PM

Moroccan Soup

1. Moroccan Soup: read recipe, sounded good, thought about it for a week. Told Winos that I would make it. Forgot grocery list for store but bought lemon, garlic, cauliflower, carrots, onions and cilantro. Congratulated self on memory. At home checked spices in drawer … turmeric, cumin, cinnamon, and cardamom. This would be fun. Sounded simple: 1-hour prep and 4–5 hours cook time.

2. Wrestled dusty crockpot from back of lower cupboard. Took only three tries to get myself back in standing position. Congratulated self on physical condition. Checked recipe again. Found out it called for coriander, not cardamom. Knocked on doors of known cooks. No coriander. Looked up "what is coriander"? Found out it was a toxic poison. Checked spelling, had typed in "oleander." Corrected spelling found it was the "seeds of cilantro." Why not use fresh cilantro? Looked it up … no good. Called Helen who is a great cook, not home, left coriander message.

3. Washed dried and chopped, chopped, chopped 4 cups cauliflower, 2 cups onions, 2 cups carrots, and peeled and chopped humongous garlic cloves.

[see more]

Measured turmeric, pepper, cumin, cinnamon, and cardamom. Put them in tiny, cute dish. This is fun. Damn, used cardamom by mistake! Threw out tiny cute dish of spices. Remeasured the spices … left out cardamom. Smells good, looking forward to fragrant bowl of soup.

4. Measured 6 cups of broth and 2 cups water. While heading over to get filtered water, stepped on sticky bits of cauliflower and onions on floor. Dumped everything in crockpot, added lentils, tomatoes, tomato paste, and spices. Yum. Shoes sticking to floor, but congratulated self on job well done. Turned pot from warm to high.

5. Surveyed mess in kitchen and on floor. Realized several hours had gone by. Rinsed off cutting board and tried to figure out how to lift heavy hot crockpot enough to slide cutting board under it. Only took 15 minutes. Loaded dishwasher. Washed sticky gunk from floor and shoes. Sat down, ate two brownies. Rested. Noted time. Left apartment went down for wine with friends. Helen brings coriander, we drink to kitchen gods. Feeling better, ate snacks.

6. Back to apartment. Added coriander, stirred stuff in crockpot. Set frozen spinach to thaw in bowl. One hour later found coriander floating listlessly on top, obviously not doing its part. Lentils hard as nails. Forced coriander to bottom, stirred the lentils,

[see more]

dropped wet mass of squeezed out spinach into crockpot for last half hour per recipe. Later sampled soup. Lentils not swelled with pride as expected. Taste at best, mediocre. Re-read recipe. Soup should be better next day. Dumped it into two big pans to cool. Still hopeful. Ate peanut butter toast and cocoa for supper. Jammed cooled vats of soup in refrigerator at 9 pm. Sat down, put feet on ottoman, yelled at politics on TV, ate another brownie.

7. At 11:00 pm turned on dishwasher, noted I bought wrong dishwasher soap, hoped for the best. Bad timing on dishwasher, loud clunking. Could not sleep. Passed out at midnight.

8. Next day refrigerator smells like garlic. Removed heavy pans of cold soup. Heated one bowl of soup, added lemon and cilantro. Tried to eat it. Nothing-helps.

9. Plan B: will fill baggies with soup, place them flat to freeze them, then stand them up like little soldiers in freezer to eat in times of desperation. Might taste better with coconut milk added. Ever hopeful.

10. Filled bags with soup. Laid them flat to freeze. In the evening found one bag not properly sealed. Scrubbed out frozen soup from all over freezer and rescrubbed floor. Sat down, put feet on ottoman, ate rest of brownies, drank wine, yelled at TV.

👍 Like   💬 Comment   ↪ Share

Joyce Gross
May 1 at 6:24AM

Child Care

Guess what I got just now? There was a knock on my door. I opened it to see a dozen toddlers outside my apartment. A little guy named Charlie was holding a May basket filled with candy made out of a crayoned coffee filter with a ribbon handle. Happy May Day!

They are part of more than a hundred children from eight weeks thru four years of age who attend day care here at our establishment. These children interact with their Grandfriends by sharing arts and crafts music pancake day and so much more.

Wouldn't you like to be able to go over and rock a baby for twenty minutes or listen to voices of little children playing outside when you are in your 80s and 90s and have absolutely no responsibility for their care? Perfect!

👍 **Like**   💬 **Comment**   ↪ **Share**

Joyce Gross
May 5 at 12:24PM

Culture Shock: Learning When Old
We have many attendants from another continent who care for us. We asked them to share their culture with us on a program we devised and called African Culture Day. Our part time minister Pastor G from Ghana was the MC. He told us so much about that huge continent that we did not know.

These wonderful people dressed for us in their beautiful African clothes and colorful scarves and explained to us that in their culture they consider old people to have wisdom and that they respect them and go to them for advice and counsel. Then they said, "We love old people, we love old people and it is our mission in life to care for them." Well, you can imagine the shock that was to us American residents! To top it off they served us a wonderful lunch of African foods!

No one had ever told us before that we were loved because we were old. These attendants shared with us that they were touched because no one in all their years of caring for people had ever asked them as a group to share like this. Well I guess we are never too old to learn about love in any culture!

 Like    Comment   Share

Joyce Gross
May 8 at 7:02PM

Soap Operas

My watching soap operas is all my mother's fault. Rose listened to the radio's "Oxydol's Own Ma Perkins" and "The Guiding Light." That was followed by the mournful tones of "The Red River Valley" and the announcer saying, "We present Our Gal Sunday, the story of an orphan girl from a small mining town in the West who found true happiness with one of England's most handsome Lords, Lord Henry Brinthrope!" Who could resist that?

So, I heard The Guiding light for years and then it came on television! There were year- long gaps in my viewing due to getting educated, married and babies, and stuff. But I was always able to follow the adventures of the heroine Reva Shane and her multiple marriages. I will never forget her classic scene where she threw herself into the town water fountain, declared herself baptized, and named herself the Slut of Springfield. I remember she was wearing a red dress. Over the years she became Reva Shane, Lewis, Lewis, Lewis, Spaulding, Lewis, Winslow, Cooper, Lewis, and Lewis O'Neil. So, I consider myself something of an expert on Soaps.

1. If you see a wedding dress before the wedding, the wedding will never happen.

[see more]

2. Whenever the camera scans a scene with a door in it someone will burst through.

3. Sometimes characters go away for a while and come back completely different people. You pretend you don't notice the switch.

4. Young children always go away to boarding school and come back as 20-year olds wanting to go into the family business.

5. Lead characters go into life-threatening, heartbreaking situations every day and comas when their contracts are being renegotiated. Why do we watch as old people? Because we knew all these people when they were young, and we want to see how their grandchildren turned out!

👍 **Like**   💬 **Comment**   ↪ **Share**

Joyce Gross
May 15 at 8:41AM

Elegant Dinners

Every other month we have an elegant dinner. The chef gets to display his talents in planning and pulling off a spectacular meal with a fancy dessert. Some men who vowed that when they retired, they would never again wear a suit jacket relent and do so. One year one of the men actually wore a tuxedo for the Christmas elegant dinner.

As for the women, they wear their Grandmother of the bride dress that they thought they would never wear again. The jewelry that has been hidden in places no one would ever find sparkle on their hands if they can get it over that knuckle. If not, it goes on a chain around the neck. Lovely music from a string quartet entertains us and the tinkle of glasses of wine and lovely food and dessert are so enjoyable.

Some of us close our eyes and remember other times and other places we celebrated with people we loved. Then on to the club room for an after-dinner drink. Best of all when it is over, we do not have to toddle outside in the cold or dark and drive anywhere. We take the elevator!

 Like    Comment   Share

Joyce Gross
May 20 at 10:12PM

Steps

What is all this craziness about counting steps? Who is doing ten thousand steps a day? I did actually count as I walked outside around my building this evening. It was about seven hundred steps. So, I walked around it three times for 2100 steps. How many should I do at my age?

I do walk to the elevator several times a day. Come to think of it, Emma who is 99 walks with her walker all day starting after breakfast. Do I want to get to 98? I have always been of the opinion that nothing good happens after 90. One year away. I better get this book done!

 Like   Comment   Share

Joyce Gross
May 29 at 4:49PM

Washing Clothes for Grandma Rose
When my mother was old, I used to wash clothes for her. Every time I found shredded Kleenex in the washer and dryer. I never could figure out where it came from. Now I am washing clothes for another old person, myself. I have finally solved it. We women do not carry purses inside our buildings. We tuck Kleenex in our folded-up blouse sleeves, and it comes out in the washer and dryer. It's an old lady thing!

👍 Like   💬 Comment   ↪ Share

Joyce Gross
June 2 at 11:19AM

Communicating When Old

Almost all the residents here hate technology. We continually call our grandchildren to help us with it. However, we residents communicate with each other by a not-so-secret method.

We have a metal door frame outside our apartment door. It has a clip on it. We communicate by placing notes, birthday cards, get well cards, invites and thank you notes in the clip. We also communicate in a secret language soon to be extinct. Cursive!

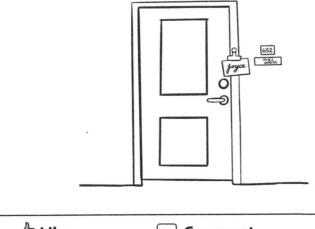

👍 **Like**   💬 **Comment**   ↱ **Share**

Joyce Gross
June 6 at 3:37PM

Thank God for Ipad

As I write my posts on my iPad while watching TV, I complete my thoughts about a particular subject and send it off to my son Patrick who supposedly edits it (it doesn't need much). Occasionally I forget what I sent so I have to search through my "sent" email or ask Pat what I sent. He thinks it is funny since we are at the Lake in Minnesota and he is sitting across from me editing a book for someone else!

👍 Like   💬 Comment   ↪ Share

Joyce Gross
June 14 at 5:06PM

Art Appreciation for Old People

I have not had a lot of success in persuading other people to appreciate art as I do. When our children were young, I could check out framed pictures for three weeks from the library. I am sure I talked about each painting and the artist, but everything is a blur now because we were raising seven kids.

I do have a clear memory of being a Picture Lady and taking pictures to school. I have retained this memory of Van Gogh's Sunflowers or was it Starry Night … I remember part of my shtick was playing Starry Starry Night on a tape. My number six and seven children (twins) were mortified that I was coming to their classroom to embarrass them. Now that they are 52 one of them mentioned that I was actually OK, and he remembered the song.

I thought the residents here should have a similar experience, so I persuaded our Recreation Director to work with me to feature an artist every month and show his or her work in the Arts and Crafts Room. We've had it for nearly a month, and it needs a little tweaking, but I know that next month will be even better because I'll be playing Starry Starry Night on a loop or something which I will figure out by next month.

 Like    Comment   Share

Joyce Gross
June 19 at 9:15AM

The Egg and I

Excitement at Breakfast. In 1945, a humorous popular book called The Egg And I was published and in high school three years later I wrote a supposedly humorous editorial called "The Leg and I" about the brand new idea of Bermuda shorts for men. But today I have returned to the Egg and I because of what happened at breakfast.

As you may or may not know we have a bowl of shelled hard-boiled cold eggs available for our continental breakfast each morning along with fresh fruit, cold and hot cereal, pastries, toast, juices and coffee (I know, Senior Living, right?). Anyway, the woman next to me at our cozy table for six, had her egg warmed up in the microwave. There it was sitting in its bowl at the table all innocent looking. She stuck a fork in it and it exploded all over us!

Turns out 45 seconds in the microwave is too long! Who knew?

 Like    Comment   Share

Joyce Gross
June 23 at 7:42PM

Keeping Healthy

I used to be 5'4". My height allowed my weight to be normal. Now that I am slightly compressed, well 5'2", I am still everything I was at 5'4" but suddenly I am overweight? This is not fair. My son tried to explain to me about height-based weight something or other. So, I said to him "was I also overweight at 8 pounds 3 ounces at birth when I was only 20 inches tall? He could not answer me. I get a lot of that as I age. Sometimes my kids seem baffled by my observations.

Did you know that merely standing up and placing your palms forward as your arms are hanging down improves your posture and may add inches to your height? In the class that I attended on "Posture" we residents practiced ears over shoulders, shoulders over hips and palms forward. We look strange as we walk around the building, but I can hardly wait until my grandkids all hunched over their devices see me at 5'4" again!

👍 **Like**   💬 **Comment**   ↪ **Share**

Joyce Gross
June 28 at 10:39AM

Telephones

Ever since I gave up my landline, I have been getting complaints from my children. They expect me to carry my cell phone around all the time like they do. I told them I treat my mobile phone like my landline, which also had a recording device, and that I would get back to them in due time. Carrying it around all the time could make a person nervous. They don't get it. I fear that they have become brainwashed by Technology!

As for the grandchildren, I saw on TV the other day a segment of young people trying to figure out how to dial a number on a telephone with a detached receiver. They could not figure out how to pick it up. To top it all off I saw my great grandson who was 2 try to talk with his daddy on the TV remote!

 Like   Comment   Share

Joyce Gross
July 2 at 12:26PM

How Late is too Late?
Over the years I have tried to lose pounds while still in-
dulging in the foods I like. It has never worked. The ci-
der-vinegar diet, the protein diet, every-other-day diet,
not one of them caused weight loss.

Now that my waist has disappeared but not forgotten
and everything is lower and wider, I am thinking I must
try the Diet of Last Resort, so I will just give up carbs for a
day then a week and then a month. Probably easy.

Did I tell you about the fresh ground coffee and out of the
oven cookies all day long at my establishment? Some-
body said they have fruit right next to the cookies.

👍 **Like**   💬 **Comment**   ↪ **Share**

Joyce Gross
July 7 at 5:12PM

Recipes
I just sorted through some of my favorite recipes and tried to figure out who I could persuade to make one of them, maybe even the wonderful soup I was always going to make but never did. I will then ask that person, most likely a relative, to try the recipe and freeze some of it for me.

We old people are sometimes surprisingly cunning yet highly adaptive.

👍 Like   💬 Comment   ↗ Share

Joyce Gross
July 12 at 2:13PM

What Do Old People Do Every Day?
I am sure you remember Mavis who dusts her car, a
27-year-old Lexus with 190,000 miles on it. She went
shopping at the Dollar Store and when she left, she ac-
cidentally grazed the fender of her car against the fender of the car next to her. She got out, checked both cars,
and seeing no damage drove out of the parking area as
another car was driving in.

She went grocery shopping and started feeling guilty.
She went back to the Dollar Store to see if she could
find out the car's owner. She saw a note on the car she
had hit. She read it and it said "an old lady hit your car
and drove off. Call me" and left a phone number. She
checked in the Dollar Store but did not find the owner.
She took the note from the car, drove to the police
station, and turned herself in.

The policeman wrote down the whole long story and
went outside and got her license number from her car.
That made her nervous, so she asked him if she did
anything wrong? He said "yes" because she had taken a
note that did not belong to her from someone's car. He
told her that she should follow him back to the Dollar
Store. He got there faster and by the time she got there
he was walking out with the woman who worked in the
back room of the Dollar Store. The woman said the car

[see more]

actually belonged to her dad and it was all dented up anyway, so the fender scrape was no big deal and then she and Mavis hugged and now they are good friends. Hours had passed. Mavis learned not to take notes off other people's cars. The policeman shook his head. So that is what old people do all day. They make friends.

👍 **Like**　　　　💬 **Comment**　　　　↪ **Share**

Joyce Gross
July 15 at 10:20AM

Swiss Chard

I was told by my doctor that I need to eat more greens. I was not surprised as I had asked a Chinese friend why the women in her family lived well into their 100s. She said, "They eat greens." She asked what greens I ate, and she actually laughed when I said, "string beans."

She told me nettles were growing right now in the ditches in my city and dandelion greens were readily available and why was I not taking advantage of these?

So, I bought Swiss Chard and I am hoping it dies in my fridge before I have to cook it. I also heard that you can get supplements called "greens something" that contains 20 servings of greens in each scoop and you can hide it in a smoothie.

 Like    **Comment**   **Share**

Joyce Gross
July 19 at 5:08PM

Exercise in Your 90s

Let's face it, so many Seniors hate to exercise. Many of those who have never exercised and not died from it live here. When you are 90 and looking for your next milestone of 100 it focuses your mind. Many are from the school of "I never exercised in my life so why start now" philosophy but some who now have their very own exercise room embrace it. And then there are those who regularly exercised and still want to. Bless their hearts.

So, I interviewed some 90 plus year olds.

May … age 99.

She walks all day with her walker chatting with people going to meals, engaging all day long. Never exercised. She has never taken a pill in her life, although now admits to taking a baby aspirin. She is slim, eats her meals with gusto, and says she is so fortunate she does not have to cook anymore.

David ... age 96

He had a new hip put in a few months ago. He was up walking the next day. He used to swim every day and now has no pool here. He goes to exercise daily and

[see more]

uses hand and leg weights. Just got back from a four-day family wedding in another state and recommends wheelchair service in airports for gate hopping.

Violet … age 93.

She spends one half hour a day walking on a treadmill. Admits to being a bit confused awhile back but now has a pacemaker and is back to driving, shopping, and cooking.

There are four or five of us who graduated from high school in 1948. We will all be 90 in 2020. I might let you know how it goes.

 Like    Comment   Share

Joyce Gross
July 22 at 9:00AM

Who is Betraying Me Now?

When you are old and wake up in the morning you may not know what day it is much less what time it is. I recommend a mobile phone to orient you, but first put on your glasses.

Then it's time for the body check to see which limbs (legs and arms to you youngsters) and joints are betraying you. When that is done, take three deep breaths and sit up on the side of your bed for one minute. If everything is in sync get up and prepare for another day.

Never under any circumstances jump out of bed. Your body won't work that way anymore.

👍 **Like**   💬 **Comment**   ↪ **Share**

Joyce Gross
August 3 at 11:22AM

Chair Ballet

Who knew we could perform ballet in a chair? I found out how last Monday. Our usual practice of using 3-pound weights was interrupted by our instructor's introduction of a lovely ballet teacher. Before we knew it, we were lifting our arms as high as we could and swaying and pointing our toes out at angles and bringing our feet back gracefully. We bent forward at angles previously unknown to us and in all these glorious movements we were listening to beautiful music.

Although it is a little late for a career change for me, I think I should go for it. Next week I will try it standing up.

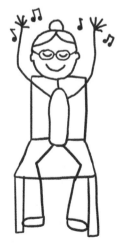

 Like    Comment   Share

Joyce Gross
August 12 at 6:34PM

Aquarium Update: How Seniors Amuse Themselves
We first had only six fish. Now we have over twenty, not teeny baby fish but adults in various colors added by aquarium people. Today after breakfast I stopped by to see the new fish. There were two of them. I squeezed along the side hoping to see behind the coral to find where they were hiding. Suddenly all twenty of the fish charged at me. They were frenzied. I was startled so I left.

After exercise class I squeezed by the side and looked, the fish totally ignored me and hid behind the coral.

At five thirty I approached the side of the tank. All twenty frenzied fish charged straight at me again. It was weird!

I finally figured it out. If I want fish to come to me, I have to press against the tank wearing my beige blouse with the small black dots. The one that looks like fish food.

👍 **Like**   💬 **Comment**   ↗ **Share**

Joyce Gross
August 16 at 7:19AM

Missing Balls
In my effort to use environmentally friendly solutions
I purchased three wool balls. They're designed to put
in the dryer to soften clothes instead of using softener
sheets. They have been noisily doing their job ever since
I bought them.

Today I washed a very small load and threw it into the
dryer. It was so noisy I checked and could find only one
ball. Where were the others?

Then I remembered that I had washed sheets the day
before. I investigated. That same fitted sheet that tries
to kill me every time I try to put it on the bed stole my
balls and cleverly concealed them in its deep corner
pockets. Hiding on the shelf in my closet it had seemed
a little bulky when I folded it. Martha Stewart would
probably faint.

👍 **Like**　　　　　💬 **Comment**　　　　　↪ **Share**

Joyce Gross
August 21 at 8:07PM

The First Thing I Wrote that I Got Paid For
The following is a copy of a letter I wrote after purchasing non-gluten hamburger buns for the first time.

Dear Person

Although your cupcakes are actually quite good, your hamburger buns leave a lot to be desired. They are dry and crumbly and fail to support the weight of the hamburger, which honestly was not that large. Adding catsup and mustard and a little mayo resulted in my holding the messy burger in my bare hands as the bun had totally disintegrated. Ingeniously, I managed to wrap the whole mess in the by-now wilted lettuce. Thank you for the experience as I had never eaten a hamburger that way before. Oh, and the buns cost $4.49. I noticed the price as I slipped the remainders into the refuse.

Very Truly Yours,

Joyce Gross, age 89

PS. I received a $20 reimbursement check from the nice owner of the company.

PPS. I also received a letter explaining that the buns should be purchased from the freezer and kept frozen and removed one at a time for eating. Who knew?

👍 **Like**   💬 **Comment**   ↪ **Share**

Joyce Gross
August 28 at 2:16PM

Influential Book
I asked a friend if he had ever read a book that influenced him for the rest of his life. He said he had. The book influenced him so much that he chose the subject as his life's career.

My experience was different. I read a book called Cheaper by the Dozen when I was young. As I recall it was the story of a blended family of a dozen children. The father was an engineer of some sort whose job was trying to find the least amount of motion for any given task. His idea for his family was when they dried after a shower, they should come up one side of their body with a towel and go down the other side. It haunts me as I have tried and never succeeded in doing this right, but think of it every damn time I step out of the damn shower.

 Like    Comment   Share

Joyce Gross
August 31 at 6:27PM

Eyeball Danger
Well it finally happened. I was reading a magazine and looking at a small picture when I put my fingers on the picture and tried to widen it. Last night when I shut my eyes, I saw words go by on my eyelids and I actually could read the type. Also, when I was playing a lot of Words with Friends I gazed up at the ceiling and there was the grid and I was spelling words on it.

When my kids were young, I warned them that too much TV would result in TV eyeballs.

Good Lord, I have iPad iBalls!

👍 **Like**   💬 **Comment**   ↪ **Share**

Joyce Gross
September 1 at 6:45PM

Compression Stockings
My doctor informed me that he was changing my blood pressure meds and that I would now need to wear compression stockings! Have you ever tried to get those things on?

When I was a nurse, I used to put them on other people. No problem since there is a way to do it known to medical people. I still fancy myself a medical person. It is, however, totally different putting them on yourself! I will be discussing BP medications on my next doctor visit although someone at breakfast today mentioned this torture hosiery now can be purchased with zippers.

👍 **Like**   💬 **Comment**   ↗ **Share**

Joyce Gross
September 4 at 3:52PM

Gluten-free spaghetti

Non-gluten spaghetti has a mind of its own. It does not lie there placidly waiting for the sauce. It reaches out and grabs it and then decides it does not want it and sloughs it off and lies there naked on your plate. Each strand strikes a pose and refuses to embrace the sauce.

I froze the leftover spaghetti. When it thawed, I tried to fork it out of the bag into the bowl. Each strand was independent and refused to touch any other strand. Some of it stood upright at an angle. Nevertheless, I poured sauce on it and put it in the microwave and when it came out, I cut its wild exuberance into small pieces and ate it with a tablespoon. I refuse to be bested by a noodle.

👍 **Like**   💬 **Comment**   ↪ **Share**

Joyce Gross
September 10 at 7:15AM

Ballet
Yes, it can be done by a bunch of old people especially if led by a young beautiful volunteer ballerina. She has us raise our arms ever so gracefully over our heads and then bring them down ever so gently like feathers in a breeze. Then deep breaths with the arms up and gently down. And now the legs. Both legs together. Point the toe to the side and return, now the other toe to the side and return and the beautiful music, and the arms and the legs and we feel like we are transported. Our eyes are closed, and we are carried away by the music for a whole half hour. She promised that in a few months we shall try it standing up.

👍 **Like**   💬 **Comment**   ↷ **Share**

Joyce Gross
September 26 at 8:35AM

Hibernation

It took the people in Minnesota a long time to come out of hibernation this year. There was that three-day snow-storm on April 15th, and everybody was wretched. I had five calls from old friends, and we promised to meet after Easter if the snow was gone. What with one thing or the other, lunching will have to wait because every-body is "up north" which means cabin season on any of 10,000 lakes. Opening up the cabin is a ritual that sometimes stretches into weeks. The chances of your friends being at the same lake at the same time as you are slim. We will definitely meet for lunch in the Fall right after closing up the cabin happens and before the snow starts again.

👍 **Like**   💬 **Comment**   ↪ **Share**

Joyce Gross
September 30 at 6:40AM

September 30th

This morning at breakfast I told everybody that it was HATH day today. Nobody knew what I was talking about. You know "Thirty days HATH September," I explained. I thinkith it wath funny!

 Like    Comment   Share

Joyce Gross
Ocotber 2 at 10:02PM

Swim Meets

I love going to my grandchildren's sporting endeavors. Over the years I've spent many hours watching my children and now grandchildren in baseball, soccer, football, track, cross country, skiing, basketball, gymnastics, dance, and swimming events.

Just last Thursday I went to my granddaughter's swim meet. It is October in Minnesota and the day was windy and 35 degrees and we dressed for it. We arrived at the high school and the pool is on the ground level but as you know the benches are raised around the pool and the higher you go to sit, the warmer it gets.

About an hour and a half into it, my daughter in law and I were red faced and sweating. I was using the program for a fan and she was regretting the wool socks she put on in the morning, especially since she was having hot flashes. No wonder they call the different swimming sections HEATS!

Later my granddaughter thanked me for coming, and she did swim so well. I always thought I would walk through hot coals to watch my kids and grandkids perform … and when I think about it, I kind of did.

👍 **Like**   💬 **Comment**   ↪ **Share**

Joyce Gross
October 8 at 12:31PM

Apple Watch
I was awakened at 4:16 the other morning by a squeaky little voice saying, "Good morning, pal. It's 4:16." I had inadvertently switched my watch face to the Mickey Mouse one in my sleep.

My watch has been one of the best presents I ever got and is a continual source of amusement to me. At breakfast one day in winter the women were arguing about the temperature. I calmly asked Siri what the temperature was.

"It is 6 degrees," she said. That settled that. "How many calories in a donut" or in a game of scrabble, "How do you spell adjunct?" Siri has become the arbiter of all things. I continue to marvel at her knowledge. And how about that flashlight in the middle of the night?

 Like    Comment   Share

Joyce Gross
October 16 at 9:12AM

Parathyroidectomy

Yes, I had surgery on my parathyroid. I had to diagnose the condition myself as my doctors here did not agree with me and two doctors told me I was too old to have surgery. Eighty-nine is not too old. I flew on a Wednesday to the clinic where the best surgeons are. Had surgery on Thursday and flew home Friday. All my bad symptoms are gone, and my energy is back. I am now the only one in senior living who is actually getting younger! Here's to you Dr. M. You are kind of young, but you know what you're doing!

👍 Like   💬 Comment   ↷ Share

Joyce Gross
October 20 at 8:42PM

Track Meet I was so thrilled to go to my grandson's all college cross country track meet. The whole pack of them ran an 8K ... it was 90 degrees with 65% humidity.

Note to self: Do not wear jeans with support hose when temp is over 75 degrees.

👍 **Like**   💬 **Comment**   ↪ **Share**

Joyce Gross
October 27 at 6:46PM

Fire Alarm
At 7:15 last night I came into my apartment and heard my smoke alarm dinging. I called the person who replaces the batteries in it. When they got there the dinging had stopped. They replaced the batteries anyway.

At 7:12 this morning my alarm started ringing. It sounded suspiciously like my smoke alarm. Oh.

👍 **Like**   💬 **Comment**   ↪ **Share**

Joyce Gross
October 29 at 10:10AM

Jelly Beans

I absolutely love jellybeans. This past month I had given up sugar. It was more or less an experiment to see if I could do it and what effect it had on my body. It had one effect so the other night I picked up jelly beans one by one from a table and I savored each individual taste—lime, strawberry, licorice, peppermint and then I picked up a clear tasteless one, I couldn't figure it out and that is when I woke up.

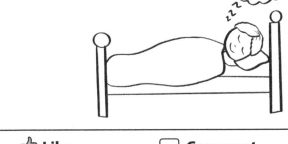

 Like   Comment   Share

Joyce Gross
October 31 at 9:45AM

Halloween

Because I am expected at breakfast every morning at 8:00 a.m., people get nervous when I don't show up. We have a little clip for messages on the frame outside the door.

I put a note on the clip that said "SLEEPING." Later, when I opened the door, I was startled to see a large plastic rat hanging by the tail on my clip.

Mavis has a little haunted house for Halloween with several small figures and rats on a table by her door along with a ghost and a skull picture hanging from the door. She goes to bed early. I go by and put her rats in compromising positions or stuck in the chimney. This will probably go on till after Halloween. It is how Seniors amuse themselves.

👍 **Like**   💬 **Comment**   ↪ **Share**

Joyce Gross
November 1 at 8:18PM

Pictures
I have three pictures of myself from the 30s and 40s, a few from the high school yearbook, three from nurses training and our wedding book. I have one baby book full of pictures of our first child, l/2 baby book of the second child, 1/4 for the third child, a few of the fifth child and for the twins six and seven I had to cut a picture in half so they could each take a picture of themselves for a school project. I have 2000 pictures of our grandchildren and great grandchildren all on my computer where I probably will never see them again. What is wrong with this picture?

👍 **Like**   💬 **Comment**   ↪ **Share**

Joyce Gross
November 7 at 3:46PM

Apple Watch is Displeased

My Apple Watch is displeased with me. Just because I exercised for a whole hour yesterday it seems to think I should achieve that goal every day. It sends me little messages designed to prod me into repeating that.

It encourages me with "just 9 more minutes of brisk walking will allow you to close your circle" or you really achieved your goal yesterday, how about trying that again today?

Like "Nooo," I am still recovering from yesterday's burst of energy. I might try the breathing thing to stop it vibrating on my wrist! I am still recovering from that incident with Mickey Mouse.

👍 **Like**   💬 **Comment**   ↪ **Share**

Joyce Gross
November 14 at 5:09PM

Danger from Moving Vehicles

I thought Senior Living would be a sedate existence. That was before I experienced moving scooters and motorized wheelchairs in my living establishment. Ezra who likes to be the first one at breakfast had been in previous life a truck driver and still drives like one. He barrels down the hallway and has never been late for breakfast.

Helen, on the other hand, is adept at piloting her wheelchair to the table and beyond, taking the tablecloth with her as she scoots too far under the table propelling the table forward until she regains control. Best not to sit with your back to the wall when Helen arrives at the other side! However, she is the hostess with the mostess and everyone wants to be at her table. This is living on the wild side for Seniors!

👍 **Like**   💬 **Comment**   ↪ **Share**

Joyce Gross
December 3 at 7:47PM

Hail Mary
When I was in the eighth grade, I was selected to be the Virgin Mary in our annual Christmas pageant, and a boy who had a crush on me was St. Joseph. It was bad enough that a boy angel fell on his face when the angels came down the aisle and the light bulb in the manger full of straw exploded. No fire ensued in the straw, but it smelled funny. Finally, the curtain came down.

Then the most embarrassing thing happened. I glanced up at St Joseph and he was handing out cigars to the Wise Men.

 Like    Comment   Share

Joyce Gross
December20 at 2:06AM

Sleepless in Minnesota
It's 2 AM I cannot sleep
I wish I had no thoughts so deep
That keep me wide awake in bed
While thoughts go tumbling
Through my head.

So I get up and pace the floor
And think of buying gifts galore
For grandchildren daughter and 6 boys
Who no longer play with toys.

It used to be so fun to buy
But then alas the years did fly
And now my kids are getting old
And walk around and feel the cold.

But sweaters mufflers coats and scarves
Seem redundant and bizarre
When all I want is to feel the joy
Of Christmas morning and the perfect toy!

👍 Like   💬 Comment   ↱ Share

Joyce Gross
December 23 at 7:02PM

Christmas Stocking

My son John sent me pictures of his Christmas stocking. He is 58 now and lives in California and apparently is still using this stocking. It seems in an emergency sewing job I nipped a bit of red felt from the back of his Christmas stocking and later apologized by patching it and writing "I am sorry in glitter."

His stocking also got wet in a basement flooding. These are the kind of things that happen when you are raising seven children. I will never live this down as there is photographic evidence.

👍 **Like**   💬 **Comment**   ↪ **Share**

Joyce Gross
December 26 at 7:14AM

Alexa
I got Alexa for Christmas. At first, I thought she was kind of real and I kept saying please and thank you. She actually knows all the songs I know. I think she knows a great deal more than I do even though she is so much younger than I am. She is new to my apartment but keeps making suggestions on upgrading my life. She has been giving me recipes and grocery lists and turning my TV off and on and telling me jokes. I think she is better than the robot dog I was thinking of getting.

👍 **Like**   💬 **Comment**   ↪ **Share**

Joyce Gross
December 31 at 10:54PM

Widows and Widowers

I really don't like the words widow and widower but that is what the majority of us are here in Senior Living. After the shock of your husband or wife's death wears off and when you are ready to face living alone you will find it is a good place to be.

When you are trying to remember who you were in your single life 60 some years ago you will find that so many here went through this very thing and they survived and so will you.

You will find that you can laugh again at all the funny little ordinary things and life is good and you aren't alone after all. You still have your outside family and friends and your inside family will really come through for you. You will laugh again … I know this is true because it happened to me.

👍 Like   💬 Comment   ↪ Share

Made in the USA
Monee, IL
04 August 2023

40422904R00046